— James Cardinal Hickey

"Mrs. Doherty's books are always best sellers and with good reason. Her writing is clear, to the point, so that it is hard to miss what she is saying."

— *The Crux of Prayer*

"Reading Catherine Doherty's writings has always been both a pleasure and an enriching experience."

— *Spirituality Today*

"Catherine Doherty's years of total dedication to the people of God, the crosses she has carried, and the tremendous graces she has received all leave their mark on what she writes, adding new depths now to the perception which has always been hers ... a present-day prophet whose commission is validated by a long life spent in 'living the Gospel without compromise.'"

— *Sisters Today*

"Catherine Doherty has the gift of a great and joyous faith and of making life an adventure, a pilgrimage."

— Dorothy Day

Light in the Darkness

A Christian Vision
for Unstable Times

adapted from the writings of
Catherine de Hueck Doherty

MADONNA HOUSE PUBLICATIONS
Combermere, Ontario, Canada

Madonna House Publications®
2888 Dafoe Rd, RR 2
Combermere ON K0J 1L0

www.madonnahouse.org/publications

© 2009 Madonna House Publications. All rights reserved.

No part of this work may be reproduced, stored in a retrieval system or transmitted in any form or by any means, electronic, mechanical, or otherwise, without express written permission. The Our Lady of Combermere colophon is a registered trade-mark of Madonna House Publications.

First Edition

First printing, February 2, 2009

Compiled and adapted by Miriam Stulberg

Scripture texts in this work are taken from the New American Bible with Revised New Testament and Revised Psalms © 1991, 1986, 1970 Confraternity of Christian Doctrine, Washington, D.D. and are used by permission of the copyright owner. All Rights Reserved. No part of the New American Bible may be reproduced in any form without permission in writing from the Copyright owner.

Cover photo: Yellowstone National Park
             Trinity Photography: Dan and Sandy Wedel
             http://www.catholicprayerdiary.com/

Graphics by Rosalie McPhee Douthwright

This book is set in Berkeley Oldstyle, designed by Frederic W. Goudy for the University of California Press in 1938.
Headings are set in Caliban, designed by America's famous carver of inscriptions, John Benson, by writing with a blunt-point pen on rough paper.

Contents

Introduction	9
Wisdom in a Nuclear Age	15
"Am I My Brother's Keeper?"	17
Whom Shall We Worship?	19
It Begins With Us	21
Overcoming Fear	23
A Radical Solution	25
When We Don't Want God	27
Making God's Family	28
Revolution Of Love	30
Surrendering To Receive	31
Hold On To Your Saint!	32
The Martyrdom Of Loving One Another	34
Take My Yoke Upon You	36
Perfect Security	37
Conforming To The World	39
Just Anger	41
The Suffering That Transforms Us	44
How Am I To Atone?	45
On The Brink Of War	47

How Do I Know God's Will?	49
On The Other Hand	50
Involvement	51
Speaking The Truth Without Fear	52
A Day Of Terror And Tears	54
The Martyrdom Of Forgiveness	56
A Heart Of Love	58
Blessed Are The Meek	60
The Oasis Of His Heart	62
Showing The Face Of Christ	64
Offered With Christ	65
Why Can't I Pray?	66
Journey Inward	68
In The Shadow Of Death	70
The Entry Into Death Is Glorious	72
A Never-Ending Struggle	73
Restoration Of The Person	75
The Yardstick Of My Worth	77
Christian Culture	78
Christian Creativity	80
Restoration Of Knowledge	81

God's Greatest Gift	83
Faith For All Cultures	85
Growing In Faith	87
Beginning Again	89

Introduction

Catherine de Hueck Doherty (1896-1985) was a pioneer in implementing the social doctrine of the Catholic Church in the face of communism and economic and racial injustice. Being a Christian, she said, meant incarnating one's faith in every aspect of daily life. To do this, it was essential to remain rooted, through prayer, in a personal relationship with Christ.

Born in Russia to a wealthy and deeply Christian family, Catherine was married at the age of fifteen, served as a nurse in the First World War and, with her husband, fled the Bolshevik revolution, narrowly escaping death. Eventually the couple settled in Canada.

Raised in affluence, Catherine knew grinding poverty as she labored to support her ailing husband and young son. After years of painful struggle, her marriage fell apart and was later annulled by the Church.

While her economic situation improved, Catherine now heard Christ calling her to renounce everything to follow him. With the blessing of her bishop, she sold her possessions, made provisions for her son, George, and began a life of prayer and simple service to the poor in the slums of Toronto. Attracted by her example of radical Gospel living, men and women came to join her, and the apostolate of Friendship House was formed.

Catherine never operated according to a preconceived plan, but in response to the Holy Spirit speaking through people, circumstances, and what she called "the signs of the times." Those times—the 1930s—were the years of the Great Depression. The members of Friendship House begged food and clothing to share with those in need and used the social encyclicals of the popes to combat the growing communist influence.

When conflicts and misunderstandings forced Catherine to close the Toronto apostolate, she moved to Harlem, the preponderantly black section of New York City, to serve those suffering from racial discrimination. Scandalized by racial injustice, she travelled the country, challenging the complacent: "How can you call yourself a Christian and reject Christ in your brother, just because his skin is black?"

No matter how complex the social, economic, and political problems seemed,

Catherine always understood their root cause to be the failure of Christians to live the Gospel. Faith was never conceptual, but the incarnation of Christ's law of love.

When dissensions among the Friendship House staff resulted in Catherine's resignation, she and her second husband, Eddie Doherty, returned to Canada and settled in rural Ontario, in the village of Combermere. Here, in 1947, the most fruitful and lasting phase of Catherine's apostolic life, the Madonna House Apostolate, was born.

Like the two Friendship Houses, Madonna House also developed organically. Catherine responded to the needs of those in the Combermere area, first as a nurse, then through simple, neighborly forms of service. She organized a summer school for the lay apostolate, and it wasn't long before young men and women, and also Catholic priests, were asking once more to join her. A training center for the lay apostolate evolved and a community life modelled on that of Nazareth.

"The Holy Family did what all the villagers did," she would explain. "They did what you and I do. Joseph worked in his carpentry shop, earning a living for his family, teaching his craft to his foster son, who was

God; He prayed in the synagogue and sat with the elders at the gates. Our Lady cooked and cleaned, fetched water from the well, and listened to the neighbors' problems. There was nothing extraordinary about their lives—except that everything they did was extraordinary because it was done with perfect love."

In response to a suggestion from Pope Pius XII, the members of Madonna House voted in 1954 to make their vocation a permanent one with promises of poverty, chastity, and obedience.

The incarnation of the Gospel in everyday life was Catherine's answer to the growing secularization and depersonalization of Western world. The healing of each person through love, prayer, an integrated way of life, and the creation of communities of love were fundamental to a truly Christian culture. Her vision encompassed every field of human endeavor, from housework, manual labor, and farming to intellectual activity, the creative arts, and government service.

Catherine Doherty was a realist. In the course of a life that spanned most of the twentieth century, she saw clearly what happened to man and his world when he lived as if there were no God. But because she also knew what men and women could become, with and through God's grace, her outlook is anything but pessimistic. Beginning with personal conversion, she calls us to restore our lives and all creation to the Father's loving will.

Catherine died in 1985, but her insights are amazingly relevant to the dilemmas of our time. The following meditations are drawn from her talks and writings. May they light the way for our own response to the challenges that confront us.

> Miriam Stulberg
> Madonna House Apostolate
> January 2009

Wisdom in a Nuclear Age

In our midst is an apple tree; its fruit is golden. A voice whispers, "Help yourself and you will be like God!"

In our midst is a stable, and in the stable is a Child who came to bring us love such as we never dreamed existed.

He said, "I have come to serve." (cf. Lk 22:27) He said, "Without me you can do nothing," (cf. Jn 15:5) and "Unless you change and become like little children, you will never enter the kingdom of heaven." (Mt 18:3)

Will we follow him across Palestine? Will we listen to the wind bring his words to our century? Are we ready to hear the sounds of his Passion?

Will I give you the fruit of the apple tree, or will I take you by the hand to a stable? Will I use many words, or will I take us both to the foot of the Cross? The greatest of dialogues is between two crucified people, but crucifixion is never the end; it is always the beginning.

He came to show us how to love God and each other. Shaping the future means that I become an icon of Christ, so that when you look at my face, you know you are loved.

The future lies in our hands. Is it a golden apple, terrible but attractive, or is it a Child you will hold? With all my heart, and with all my humble prayers, I wish you the Child.

LORD, my heart is not proud;
nor are my eyes haughty.
I do not busy myself with great matters,
with things too sublime for me.

— Ps 131 —

"Am I My Brother's Keeper?"

God asked Cain, "Where is your brother, Abel?" Cain answered, "Am I my brother's keeper?"

Cain slew his brother because he envied him. We kill our brethren not because of envy, but because of avarice and greed.

Am I my brother's keeper? If we truly examined our Western consciences, we should be trembling, for indeed we have slain our brothers by enlarging our profits.

We have left them in a state where no one can envy them, paying pennies for raw products and charging dollars for the processed goods. Wearing masks of charity, we bestow a few millions, or even a billion or two that we can easily afford, but which will not alleviate the misery.

Thousands of death-dealing weapons are being sold by the affluent countries of the West. Am I my brother's keeper? No, I am my brother's killer!

And yet our desire for a life-style almost barbarous in its hedonism begets a guilt that will not allow us to be at peace.

Am I my brother's keeper? On this question hinges our political, economic, and individual survival.

"Amen, I say to you, what you did not do for one of these least ones, you did not do for me."

— Mt 25: 45 —

Whom Shall We Worship?

Ours is an era of self-deification. Technologically, we have reached supreme heights, but as we conquer space and time, we are destroying our planet.

The western world, for which nothing is sacred, is encircled with hate and destruction. We go to sleep wondering if our cities will be attacked. We are afraid to go in planes. We are afraid to go in buses. And the water isn't safe to drink!

How long will we be able to live in this polluted world we have created?

Isn't it time we fell on our knees and, turning once again to the only true God, asked him to cleanse us from our leprosy of mind and heart?

Christ calls each of us directly, and in his call there is no compromise: "Anyone who is not with me is against me." (Mt 12:30) He told us to love one another.

Love alone can bring about the salvation of the world.

"You are my friends if you do what I command you… It was not you who chose me, but I who chose you and appointed you to go and bear fruit that will remain…"

— Jn 15: 14, 16 —

It Begins With Us

My heart is breaking over the state of the world. We have, in a manner of speaking, sold our soul to the devil. We wanted to do what we wanted to do when we wanted to do it. We were interested only in ourselves.

"This is *our* gold, *our* oil, *our* water, *our* electricity," we say. When nations and individuals reach that stage, they fall apart because the greatest sin before God is pride, and avarice is its handmaid. To grab for myself that which belongs to all is a grave and tragic sin.

We are secure in our selfishness. We have grown used to our anxieties. We do not want to mature, to accept the awesome, terrible, yet totally liberating freedom that comes when we begin to incarnate Christ's law of love.

We need to gather into the barns of our heart that which will feed people, even beyond bread—God's peace, forgiveness, understanding, and joy. We have to fill our hearts with these so that people can come to us for faith, hope, and love in order to survive.

Let us put our hand to the plow. It has to begin with us.

Unless the LORD build the house,
they labor in vain who build.
Unless the LORD guard the city,
in vain does the guard keep watch.

— Ps 127: 1 —

Overcoming Fear

Courage is not the absence of fear, but fear overcome by faith. Fear is exorcised by two things: prayer and forgiveness. And the first person we need to forgive is ourselves.

"No one can have greater love than to lay down his life for his friends." (Jn 15:13) "Perfect love drives out fear." (1 Jn 4:18) Perfect love lays down its life.

If we allow fear to dominate us, then, indeed, those who have the power to kill our bodies will also have the power to kill our souls. We shall have given them that power.

To be a Christian is to risk everything including our life. It is to enter a no-man's-land where we are ridiculed, rejected, misunderstood, maligned, persecuted. We have to walk in Christ's footsteps. Because we love him, nothing will make us deviate.

We stand on a very narrow precipice. On either side is an abyss. Which way shall we move? Along the edge of faith, hope, and love?

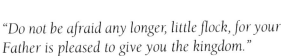

"Do not be afraid any longer, little flock, for your Father is pleased to give you the kingdom."

— Lk 12: 32 —

A Radical Solution

The Gospel demands of us what no political program could ever require—sacrifice and renunciation. A simple life-style might seem absurd, but it is the answer.

Detachment from possessions is essential, but strangely enough, whenever you think you are totally detached, you discover an abyss of attachments. How easily we are fooled!

Our lives must be a continual inner stripping. This involves relinquishing our own will. In this way, we can identify with the poor of the world and with Christ, who was stripped for our sake.

Once you accept your own poverty before God, this truth will make you free to love and to serve.

Our repentance must take the form of asceticism. This means self-discipline for the sake of God and his law. But neither asceticism nor penance is worth anything unless it is the fruit of love. Unless each of us prays and fasts, the necessary sacrifices will never materialize, and our nation may continue to consider itself the master of heaven and earth.

" ...from the person who takes your cloak, do not withhold even your tunic."

— Lk 6: 29 —

When We Don't Want God

The moment we commit ourselves to follow Christ, we enter the land of pain, because we enter his pain. We enter the pain of humanity and our own pain.

Sometimes we don't want to be like God; we don't want to touch him! We wish that Christ had been born in a different way. We wish that he hadn't died on a cross.

But he did.

"For whoever wishes to save his life will lose it, but whoever loses his life for my sake will save it. What profit is there for one to gain the whole world yet lose or forfeit himself?"

— Lk 9: 24-25 —

Making God's Family

How is a community of love formed? I have often been asked this question.

I consider St. Paul's beautiful hymn to charity in the 13th chapter of 1Corinthians to be the essence, the base, the cornerstone of a community of love. But even before St. Paul wrote those words, Christ had spoken very clearly about love:

"This is how all will know that you are my disciples, if you have love for one another." (Jn 13:35).

"I give you a new commandment: love one another. As I have loved you, so you also should love one another." (Jn 13:34)

No matter how long or how many times I meditate on that Gospel passage, I am overawed by it. God seems to ask the impossible. We, who are called to be his followers, are asked to love one another with his heart! How can an ordinary person love with the heart of God?

Nevertheless, this kind of love is the answer to all the questioning, confusion, turmoil and unrest, which are presently shaking us like bruised reeds.

First, foremost, and last, before we talk about techniques, sensitivity courses, interpersonal relationships and all the rest, we must ask ourselves the following question: Have we begun to love the people in the community in which God has placed us?

It may be a family, a lay apostolic community, a religious community, the parish, a village, a neighborhood. Have we begun to love the people with whom we live? Have I begun to be concerned, not about myself, but about everyone else?

Unless I do this, everything else will be chaff in the wind.

…if I have all faith so as to move mountains but do not have love, I am nothing…

So faith, hope, love remain, these three; but the greatest of these is love.

— 1 Cor 13: 2 & 13 —

Revolution Of Love

Is it possible to love all humanity?

Christ didn't mean we had to like everyone. "Liking" is an emotion, while "love" is a Person. Love is God. If we allow emotion to guide us in the choice of whom we are going to love, then we end up loving no one except (perhaps) ourselves, and in the wrong way.

Christ told us to love one another as he loved us. We too are called to love all men and women: those we like, those we dislike, even those who wish us evil.

The law of love demands that we become people of the towel and the water; that we, like Christ, wash our neighbor's feet. This is the true revolution that will change the face of the earth.

"For if you love those who love you, what credit is that to you? Even sinners love those who love them… But rather, love your enemies and do good to them, and lend expecting nothing back…"

— Lk 6: 32, 35 —

Surrendering To Receive

Martyrdom has various faces. St. Stephen was a bloody martyr, but I don't think this is what God intends for most of us. I think he calls us to surrender our will to him.

The word "surrender" is often understood in a negative sense. When I asked somebody what she thought "surrender" was, she thought it meant "giving up."

But surrender is not only giving up; it also means receiving. For the little I give up, I receive an awful lot. If I surrender to Christ, I receive God!

"…I came down from heaven not to do my own will but the will of the one who sent me."

— Jn 6: 38 —

Hold On To Your Saint!

That we are entering an age of martyrdom must be obvious to anybody with a nose on their face and eyes in their head! When it comes, the name of God, Our Lady, and your patron saint should be on your lips. Your patron saint is very close to you, a creature like you.

What characterizes a saint?

A saint is a lover of God; that is, a lover of all human beings.

A saint listens to the Lord and lets his words penetrate the heart. He doesn't respond with "if"s and "but"s.

The saints were free. Those who do the will of God are free, for when you do your own will, you are bound.

When you go in search of God, hold on to the hand of your saint. He or she will lead you to God as no one else can.

You are our letter, written on our hearts, known and read by all, shown to be a letter of Christ administered by us, written not in ink but by the Spirit of the living God, not on tablets of stone but on tablets that are hearts of flesh.

— 2 Cor 3: 2-3 —

The Martyrdom Of Loving One Another

Loving people whom we don't have to live with is one thing; loving those we live with is quite another! But we have to get on with it, because tomorrow or the day after, our love will be tested in the crucible of the atomic bomb, inflation, unemployment, and depression.

The other day the Secretary of the United States Treasury told the country that if the present situation continues, we will enter a world depression. I don't know if he's right, but I do know we had better enter the martyrdom of loving one another and, therefore, of truly loving God, or else we won't be able to face what's ahead of us.

If there is any encouragement in Christ, any solace in love, any participation in the Spirit, any compassion and mercy, complete my joy by

being of the same mind, with the same love, united in heart, thinking one thing.

― Phil 2: 1-2 ―

Take My Yoke Upon You

When people fear violence, they believe in what they call "law and order." They are afraid to lose the security they have acquired.

We want our little security; we want to be peaceful and quiet in a nice electric blanket, as if we were in our mother's womb. There, at least we don't have to face any difficulties.

Well, that's just plain selfish!

When you are in love with God, you cannot be at peace. You have to take upon yourself the pain, the sorrow, the fears, and the joys of the world. You have to open your heart and make room for all humanity. If you are in love with God, this becomes possible.

"For where your treasure is, there also will your heart be."

— Mt 6: 21 —

Perfect Security

We are teetering today on the edge of an abyss. In the background is the threat of terrorism. We are not secure walking the city streets. We are bewildered by the waste of world resources. Wars flare in almost every part of the world. The security to which most people cling is mere illusion.

God offers us an insecurity that leads to perfect security. His security begins when we start loving him with our whole heart, our whole mind, and our whole soul, and our neighbor as ourselves.

To love one's neighbor is the ultimate risk. It may even mean death for my brother's sake. To do this kind of loving we are given the Holy Spirit. With him, we shall have the courage to risk loving our neighbor.

Christ also asks us to love our enemies. When we obey Christ's command to love as he loved us, we have the power, the grace, and the charisms to change enemies into friends and beloved neighbors.

All this sounds very idealistic, but Christ assures us it is attainable. Through little steps taken day after day, one slowly accepts the other as he or she is and begins to love totally, tenderly, and compassionately.

...you should put away the old self of your former way of life, corrupted through deceitful desires, and be renewed in the spirit of your minds, and put on the new self, created in God's way in righteousness and holiness of truth.

— Eph 4: 22-24 —

Conforming To The World

In order to be understood and heard, must the Church conform to the world and its ideas?

If by "conform" is meant change and adaptation in order to express eternal truths in a way more understandable to modern man, the answer is "yes."

On the other hand, if it implies any compromise with the Gospel message, there can be no giving ground. Christ came to arouse us from our complacency, indifference, and hedonism so that we might follow him. The Christian and the whole Church must cry out the glad news, even if the world considers it disturbing or unpleasant. Christ came to disturb the conscience of man, and his followers must continue this mission.

Let us love the Church with a passionate love, remembering that the Church, in its sacraments and in its very being, is a mystery of love. Let us incarnate this mystery in our lives, with hearts full of charity, patience and understanding.

"…whoever lives the truth comes to the light, so that his works may be clearly seen as done in God."

— Jn 3: 21 —

Just Anger

At what point does just anger begin? At what point does a Christian lift the cords of that anger to chase the moneylenders from the temple? (cf Jn 2:13-17) When does a man reach a breaking point and begin to speak words of fire and truth to the mighty and powerful of the world?

I personally know the storms of anguish when just anger shakes one like a fever, like a fierce cold wind that makes one's teeth rattle. I knew it in the slums of Toronto during the Depression, when long queues of hungry men waited in front of our storefront. I knew it in Harlem, crying out the pain of the blacks for ten years.

I can't deny that I often used words like cords.

I am still filled with this just anger, because the face of poverty, the face of injustice, the face of man's inhumanity to man is still before me.

But at what point does this anger, this searing pain, cross a line and burst into the kind of violence we see all around us?

Christ's answer is a paradox. He says, "All who draw the sword will die by the sword," (Mt 26:52) but in another place he says, "If anyone hits you on the right cheek, offer him the other as well." (Mt 5:39) Then he picks up cords and chases the moneylenders from the temple!

How long can a Christian watch the face of the poor being ground into the dust? How long can he watch the governments of affluent nations dole out mere fistfuls of grain to the hungry when the granaries are bursting?

For myself I have only one answer: to pray unceasingly, to fast, and to remain crucified on the cross of tense, just anger. I feel safe on that strange wooden cross, for he who is nailed to it cannot succumb to the temptation of violence. A crucified person can only hang there and slowly die for those he loves.

Perhaps this is the only answer: to suffer on that cross so that hope may be born in the hearts of the poor. To suffer so that love may blossom in the hearts of the rich—a love that will reach to the very depths of the poverty of their brethren.

"In the world you will have trouble, but take courage, I have conquered the world."

— Jn 16: 33 —

The Suffering That Transforms Us

Suffering is not only physical; it can be mental or spiritual as well. In proportion to the love of God and others that grows in the soul, a massive transformation takes place through suffering. This is the threshold of a mystery into which God gently leads you.

If you follow him into his pain, it changes you. If you keep your hand in God's hand, love will grow. He who holds his hand in the hand of God knows love, for God is love.

And there, I think, is something very profound, very mysterious and deep.

...we even boast of our afflictions, knowing that affliction produces endurance, and endurance, proven character, and proven character, hope, and hope does not disappoint, because the love of God has been poured out into our hearts through the holy Spirit that has been given to us.

— Rm 5: 3-5 —

How Am I To Atone?

In her diary, Catherine reflects on her husband Eddie Doherty's absence. He was at Madonna House in Arizona for the winter; Eddie had a heart condition.

Spending more time with the Madonna House staff is a great joy, yet loneliness is not lessened, that lonely inner land in which I have been living for so long.

I have a sense that the Lord is calling me to atone. With this comes that stark realization of my unworthiness. When man offers a victim to God, it should be without blemish, but when God chooses his own victims, who can gainsay his choice? I may marvel at it or shrink, but I must joyfully obey.

So I come, Beloved, in utter simplicity. *Fiat.* Your pain in me grows and grows like a fire. My eyes seem to see so deeply into that pain of yours in others…. Give me the grace to lift that pain. To share it. Assuage it. Help it – alleviate it – and above all, atone for it.

How am I to atone? Clear and unmistakable comes the answer: *Perfect the duty of the moment, which is my will for you!* It seems so small a thing, yet it is immense too – Lord, give me the grace to do so! Please, Mary, show me how!

"...I came down from heaven not to do my own will but the will of the one who sent me."

– Jn 6: 38 –

On The Brink Of War

In October 1963, the United States learned that the Soviet Union had built nuclear missile bases in Cuba. President John F. Kennedy ordered a naval quarantine around the island to prevent the delivery of nuclear materials, and pressure was put on the Soviets to dismantle the bases. If they had not backed down, the United States would have taken military action.

In the days of the Cuban missile crisis, the whole world stood breathless, awaiting Russia's answer to the U.S. challenge. It was a moment out of time, when the world faced the possibility of nuclear war. It was a fearsome moment, and it was normal to be afraid with legitimate, human fear.

But we belong to him who is perfect love, and perfect love casts out all fear and makes the human fear of destruction and death bearable with God's grace.

The first step in such emergencies is to pray for peace, for the dark clouds to pass by, for men to keep their sanity and to remember that God exists. All day we should be beseeching the mercy of God and his intervention in human affairs.

Those of us who are far removed from the seat of the conflict must then go about our business, which is the business of God. The greatest contribution we can make is to do the duty of the moment and offer it up for our intentions. Let us be ready to serve God and our neighbor without counting the cost.

We who are strong ought to put up with the failings of the weak and not to please ourselves; let each of us please our neighbor for the good, for building up.

— Rm 15: 1-2 —

How Do I Know God's Will?

If you ask, "How do I know what God wants of me at a given time," the answer lies in the duty of the moment.

What is your next duty? It's not a question of sitting around talking about the Holy Spirit! It is getting up at night to change or feed a baby, doing the duty of a nurse or the work of a man is supporting his family. Does one like it? That depends on how much one loves!

His mother said to the servers, "Do whatever he tells you."

— Jn 2: 5 —

On The Other Hand

Do I really seek the will of God? Do I really want to live by this gentle and terrifying will?

If I go deep into my heart, I discover a strange resistance. Superficially, I still say: "I am doing God's will." Then I look again into my heart and ask myself, "Am I?"

To say I do the will of the Father and then to proceed to do my will is a sort of blasphemy. But we have to find this out ourselves. A spiritual director can help, but we have to go deep into our own hearts to really know what we're talking about.

What I do, I do not understand. For I do not do what I want, but I do what I hate.

— Rm 7: 15 —

Involvement

You have only to look at the life of Christ and our Lady to understand how little things change the world. The key is total surrender to God and faith in him.

I would like to be on the front lines, but here I am in Combermere. I am deeply attached to social justice questions and I want to keep them in my heart, but I must follow what God wants me to do at this moment. In my heart I am just as involved as before, even though I am not physically present. God has moved me to another place.

Just make the distance between your heart and your head very small, and all will be well!

"Not everyone who says to me, 'Lord, Lord,' will enter the kingdom of heaven, but only the one who does the will of my Father in heaven."

— Mt 7: 21 —

Speaking The Truth Without Fear

From a letter written by Catherine to her spiritual director in 1944.

The days to come will be very dark. Christ will be denied. Great suffering will come to his Church. And I will be called to bear some sort of witness to his verities. I have to start preparing now.

Yes, I agree with you that the greatest grace God has given me is the understanding that only a childlike faith can overcome the world. I also agree that the graces of love and poverty, and a love of the poor flow from this. Faithfulness to the Gospel, in the face of all the obstacles of human wisdom, is right also.

You ask if I would stand up and speak out against the bombing of cities in favor of a negotiated peace? Yes, I would if I were called to. But before I did so, I would have to read all that the popes wrote about war and the Mystical Body of Christ. Once convinced, I would speak without hesitation and without fear of consequences.

...living the truth in love, we should grow in every way into him who is the head, Christ...

— Eph 4: 15 —

A Day Of Terror And Tears

When I heard about Robert Kennedy being shot*, I, like everyone else, experienced a tremendous shock. I love America and the American people with a great love. To think that this beautiful nation was killing its prophets was like seeing America as a battleground of light and darkness.

My spiritual, physical, and emotional shock was so great that, frankly, I wanted to go sleep it off, to try to forget the horror of it all.

But the will of my Father was that I offer, according to the duty of the moment, that terror-filled day of pain, and of tears that wouldn't come. On that day, the duty of the moment was to begin sorting in our drama room, which was an unholy mess. So, taking myself by the scruff of the neck, I went with a few others and started sorting through boxes of costumes.

Yesterday we gathered around the statue of Our Lady of Combermere, recited the rosary, read from the Gospel, sang a few hymns, and then prayed in silence. According to the world's standard, our contribution—our atonement and even the expression of our love for the American people—did not amount to much.

But who knows what God did with that little hour spent by a group of unimportant lay apostles around a bronze statue of his Mother?

...persevere in the faith, firmly grounded, stable, and not shifting from the hope of the gospel that you heard, which has been preached to every creature under heaven...

— Col 1: 23 —

* Robert F. Kennedy, brother of assassinated American president John F. Kennedy, was shot and killed in Los Angeles on June 6, 1968.

The Martyrdom Of Forgiveness

How much faith it needs to stand before the slaughter of the innocents and still believe that the God I worship is real. Even more, my faith tells me I must love my enemies.

Most people believe we should kill our enemy. Why should I love him?

When I first began Friendship House in Harlem I started to hate white people. The more I lived with blacks in their poverty and saw the discrimination they suffered, the more I shook with what I considered to be a just hatred.

Then one day I began a retreat. I went into the church and prostrated myself. Suddenly I realized that everything I had done had been in vain. The Lord was deaf to my pleas because I hated white people. I had not fulfilled what the Russians consider to be one of the great commandments of the Lord—I had not loved my enemy. I was not at all ready to lay down my life for any white person.

I wept and wept because I had alienated myself from God.

...this is my prayer: that your love may increase ever more and more in knowledge and every kind of perception, to discern what is of value...

— Phil 1: 9-10 —

A Heart Of Love

It is good for Christians to participate in peace and protest marches, but it is utterly against the Gospel to turn peace marches into hate marches. It is good to courageously confront authority, but the way to do this is as St. Thomas More did. He spoke the truth to kings and prelates without fear, but with charity.

True nonviolence has its roots in a love that lays down its life for the other. The nonviolent must be motivated by a dream, and there must be nothing wishy-washy about that dream. They must be rooted in faith—faith in a cause, faith in a Person, faith in God. Without faith, nonviolence is impossible.

There will come a moment of choice, a moment of standing at the crossroads of a decision that may well involve life or death. To make such decisions, to be ready to lay down one's life for the other and for one's beliefs, demands violence to self.

Violence to self is to be humble, poor, meek, and pure of heart. It means to be empty of selfish motives, cleansed from everything except a burning love that will give birth to an unconquerable courage.

...draw your strength from the Lord and from his mighty power. Put on the armor of God so that you may be able to stand firm against the tactics of the devil...stand fast with your loins girded in truth, clothed with righteousness as a breastplate, and your feet shod in readiness for the gospel of peace. In all circumstances, hold faith as a shield, to quench all (the) flaming arrows of the evil one.

— Eph 6: 10-11, 14-16 —

Blessed Are The Meek

Meekness is strength. Our Lady in her meekness is like an army in battle array! Meekness can be terrifying to an opponent, since he cannot penetrate it nor get around it.

I can't think of any virtue that will exact so much from him who tries to practice it.

How the temper can flare! How my ideas have to predominate! To go around saying: "Oh, I am a sinner" doesn't get me anywhere. I have to face myself and admit: "I'm not meek at all; most of the time I'm ferocious!"

This doesn't mean that you can't express your ideas; it has to do with how you express them. It means your heart is pure. "The pure of heart shall see God," (cf Mt 5:8) and because you have seen God in this symbolic sense, you are peaceful and listening gently to what the other has to say.

Meekness means turning the other cheek. Meekness is silence before accusation. Meekness is in the words of Christ, "Father, forgive them; they do not know what they are doing." (Lk 23:34) Meekness is in the words of the old Russian man who said, after the Communists had shot the priest as he lifted the host, "Father, forgive them, *even though they know what they do.*"

Meekness is the absence of anger, but this is not won overnight. It takes courage to be meek, courage beyond our capacity. The only way to get there is by prayer.

Meekness is total reliance on God.

...living the truth in love, we should grow in every way into him who is the head, Christ...

– Eph 4: 15 –

The Oasis Of His Heart

We who walk in the desert of violence, wars, and changes that bewilder and confuse us need an oasis in which to rest and renew ourselves. Mass is the oasis to which the Good Samaritan brings us each day. Every day Christ invites us to the oasis of his heart to be refreshed there by the Wine of his compassion and love.

Love is not emotion and not a state. It is a Person – it is God himself. He is the food I receive in the Eucharistic Sacrifice. I need him daily because I am a sinner and weak. True, I am a saved sinner; but one who realizes only too well the words of Christ, "Without me, you can do nothing." (Jn 15:5) I need him, the living Bread, to love through me.

I need to participate in the daily Sacrifice of the Mass because I am in love with God. I am in love with Jesus Christ. My soul seeks union with God. It cannot rest until it finds him.

Mass is a rendezvous with Christ. Passionately in love with my God, I become one with him at the Eucharistic table.

Daily Mass is a plunging into the inexplicable, incredible mystery of love. It is a reality more real than the air I breathe, than the life I live throughout the day.

What can I bring to the world but him who has given himself to me?

My lover belongs to me and I to him...

— Sg 2: 16 —

Showing The Face Of Christ

He who eats the Bread of the Lord must in turn be "eaten up" by others. Having received God, who is love, we must give love. We who work in the front lines of spiritual warfare know that this is the only answer for a world so desperately in search of meaning.

Only when we who call ourselves Christians show the face of the resurrected Christ will seekers of God be able to see and touch him. This has to be done person to person. It cannot be done en masse. Each person needs to know that he or she is loved—loved as a friend, loved as a brother or sister in Christ. Only in the eyes of another can we find the image of Christ.

This is the commandment we have from him: whoever loves God must also love his brother.

— 1 Jn 4: 21 —

Offered With Christ

A drop of water is poured into the chalice. It represents us. We are in the chalice. And if we are the Mystical Body and the Body is offered, then in a mystical way, we too are offered.

We can offer ourselves as victims with the Great Victim. Incredible, unbelievable as it is, we can offer ourselves in atonement for our own sins and for those of others. We can make up what is lacking in the sufferings of Christ. (cf Col 1:24) Nothing is lacking in the sufferings of Christ, and yet St. Paul tells us that we are co-redeemers. In a mysterious fashion, God, in his tenderness, offers us this vision of what it means to be a member of the Body of Christ, a kingly people and a priestly people.

"…unless a grain of wheat falls to the ground and dies, it remains just a grain of wheat; but if it dies, it produces much fruit."

― Jn 12: 24 ―

Why Can't I Pray?

You have got to approach prayer as a love affair. And the accent is not on praying; it is on the one to whom you pray. You are drawn to God as a young girl is drawn to a young man. Slowly, as in a human love affair, Christ absorbs you more and more and becomes the center of your life. You savor and find new depths to every word he says.

Then you turn to the Scriptures. We call this meditation, but how can such a little word describe your plunging into the depths of each word of Christ?

As you plunge into Christ's words, your deep relationship to him, the one you call prayer, will change. You will enter into a new dimension, which some call contemplation.

What is contemplation? One Sunday I was walking in a city park, and I came across a couple sitting on a bench. Before them was their picnic basket, and a dog was happily eating their sandwiches, paper and all; I stood less than ten feet away. The two paid no attention to me, and were utterly oblivious to the dog. They were holding hands and looking at each other.

There comes a moment when words become useless—men and women just sit and look at each other. This is the moment of deepest love, when the wings of the intellect are folded and the heart is totally opened to the other. This is contemplation.

So, before you can pray, you must meet God. The best way to meet him is to stand very still, without frustration or anxiety, and wait for him. He will come if you are waiting for him.

That is really all I can tell you about prayer.

And when you hold hands with Christ, whisper my name.

My lover speaks; he says to me,
"Arise, my beloved, my beautiful one,
and come!"

— Sg 2: 10 —

Journey Inward

We must follow in the footsteps of our Brother, Jesus Christ. We must pray, beg, and implore him to let us follow him into the self-emptying that began at his birth when he took our flesh, which continued during his life in Nazareth, in his preaching, in his training a band of followers, and which was completed on the Cross when he died for love of us.

We must guard against escaping into a false or inappropriate "good." If the devil cannot tempt us with evil, he will tempt us with good. It is so much easier to get involved with the underprivileged, with world poverty, with anything except following Jesus into the fire that burns from us all that isn't of God.

But if we are leaning on, holding on to, following Jesus Christ, he will take us to the Father's heart. When we are emptied of ourselves, we will be filled with the Holy Spirit, who will teach us and reveal to us, step by step, all that we might not have understood.

Then we will fall in love with the Most Holy Trinity, and we will become part of the eternal, primary Community of Love.

"I am the way and the truth and the life. No one comes to the Father except through me."

— Jn 14: 6 —

In The Shadow Of Death

In February of 1975, Catherine received news that Fr. Eddie Doherty was dying in Arizona. Although he later recovered enough to return to Combermere, Catherine wrote this letter to the Staff about facing his death.

I accepted the news with what I hoped was great simplicity. I went back to what I was doing, namely, lunch and spiritual reading. After that I went to work on the files. I truly believe that the duty of the moment is the duty of God, and so I went about the work of my Father.

What was I feeling? It is very difficult to express. Eddie and I had already faced this contingency. I had experienced a sort of death when we took the vow of chastity, and again when he became a priest.[*] Each was a kind of detachment. The Lord was working his will in us both, and we surrendered to that will.

---

[*] Eddie and Catherine had taken a vow of chastity in 1955. In 1969 he was ordained to the priesthood in the Melkite Catholic rite. Like other Eastern rites of the Catholic Church, the Melkites have a long tradition of married clergy.

Now detachment wasn't very easy. But neither was it that difficult. It was a matter of faith. I simply share with you that when I heard of his imminent death, faith blazed in me like a sun, and I was joyous. It appeared to me that Eddie had reached the apex of his life.

A day later I phoned and heard he had improved greatly. Still, the last twenty-four hours have been somewhat momentous in my life, and I share them with you, thanking God both for the shadow of death and for Eddie's return to life.

"I will show you what someone is like who comes to me, listens to my words, and acts on them. That one is like a person building a house, who dug deeply and laid the foundation on rock..."

— Lk 6: 47-48 —

The Entry Into Death Is Glorious

Above all, we are afraid of death, of the annihilation that will someday come to us all.

Other fears beset us, but this is the root fear. The brain that functions so well, that talent that was so great, the knowledge that helped humanity in so many ways—all these will cease.

But why should I be afraid? If I have faith, the entry into death is glorious. It means being greeted by Christ himself, being *invaded* by his life, being one with him.

"*Memento mori*; remember that you must die." And it will be a joyful event, because God will greet God in me.

"'*Come, you who are blessed by my Father. Inherit the kingdom prepared for you from the foundation of the world.*'"

— Mt 25: 34 —

A Never-Ending Struggle

Perseverance is love in action, a means by which the wings of the Holy Spirit can sweep away temptations.

Perseverance says, "Be patient for just another minute. When you started out, you were in love with God—what has happened?" And the temptations curl up and depart, for what can they do against this steadfastness begotten by perseverance?

Perseverance faces life head-on. It never says, "But," or "If things were different." The language of perseverance is always a "yes" to God.

The only thing that can triumph over perseverance is when I do my own will. In the face of that kind of treatment, perseverance slowly dies. But it can be revived with one sentence: "Lord, I am sorry. Not my will, but yours."

The fight against self is never ending. Only when I am in my coffin will I be able to say I have been faithful to the end. Today I can say that by the grace of God, I have been faithful for many years, but I don't know if I am going to be faithful this Friday, or next Saturday, or Sunday! I shall only know I have persevered when I see Christ.

...let your "Yes" mean "Yes" and your "No" mean "No...
– Jm 5: 12 –

Restoration Of The Person

I believe in the restoration of the whole person through Christ. The apostle must be himself restored before he can give the Gospel message to others. This means restoration of the intellect. It means creativity and its development. It means emotional and volitional restoration. The development of manual labor skills provides a sure foundation.

My passionate desire is to develop each person to the fullness of his or her capacity and talents, to enlarge natural horizons so as to allow the supernatural ones to have room to grow and expand. In other words, to give Christ room, to give him a place within us to roam as he wishes, a place for him to breathe and stretch and grow to his full stature.

Then we can walk into the world clad in charity, truth, and humility; and we will renew it. Then we can enter into politics, economics, the latest technology, any facet of the world at large that needs restoration, for love can penetrate them all.

...that he may grant you in accord with the riches of his glory to be strengthened with power through his Spirit in the inner self, and that Christ may dwell in your hearts through faith; that you, rooted and grounded in love, may have strength to comprehend with all the holy ones what is the breadth and length and height and depth, and to know the love of Christ that surpasses knowledge, so that you may be filled with all the fullness of God.

— Eph 3: 16-19 —

The Yardstick Of My Worth

Our North American civilization judges people by what they produce. Salaries are raised in the business world according to our production: how many items have we sold? How many orders have we brought in? How many insurance policies did we sell? What were our grades in school?

Because of this yardstick, we often measure our own worth this way, as if we were extensions of machines instead of machines being extensions of us.

The incarnation, death, and resurrection of Christ are the true measure of our value. We are worth three hours of his agony on the cross. We are worth Jesus' whole life.

"For God so loved the world that he gave his only Son, so that everyone who believes in him might not perish but might have eternal life."

— Jn 3: 16 —

Christian Culture

Christian culture reflects God's penetration into all areas of human life, expresses our faith, and helps transmit it to successive generations. We are meant to attain the fullness of our humanity, permeated through and through by the presence of Christ. Each family and each Christian community is called to be a place where the human and the Christian blend, and where Christ is incarnated.

Our society is increasingly depersonalized and dehumanized. In many instances our relationships are centered on the TV, computer, and other machines, to the detriment of interpersonal relationships.

It is easy to fall into a routine of working, eating, sleeping. But we need to cultivate everything that is human: poetry, dancing, singing, painting, drama – all the arts, hospitality, helping the poor. There is nothing secular in the world, for the world has been created by God and is sacred.

Our love for God must permeate our whole life.

...whoever is in Christ is a new creation: the old things have passed away; behold, new things have come. And all this is from God...

— 2 Cor 5: 17-18 —

Christian Creativity

Beauty and creativity liberate the spirit and bring peace. They are a way to fill the other daily needs of clothing, housing, tools, food, entertainment. We have a need to bring beauty into our surroundings. Even junk can be made into beauty and waste can be restored to usefulness.

There is a loneliness of faith that comes from God, so that we might awaken to the power within us. This is a creative loneliness that makes us bring beauty and new life to others. The gift of creativity is never for oneself alone.

We are called to bring God's many-faceted beauty to the world, framed in love and peace so that it reflects his face.

God looked at everything he had made, and he found it very good.

— Gn 1: 31 —

Restoration Of Knowledge

Knowledge is given to men and women for one purpose only: that man might love God and serve him.

Our tragedy is that we have perverted that knowledge and have placed it at the service of the Prince of Darkness, bringing humanity and the world to the brink of a precipice.

Intellectual seduction is one of the greatest sins. Even when we discuss the Gospel, we rationalize. How terrible to rationalize away Christ and his commandment of love, and then influence others to do likewise!

We have one aim: that people know God, know that he loves them and that they are called to love him back. All sociology, all politics, must serve the primary good of reaching eternal life. This is the greatest good that I can wish for my neighbor. Love must be the motivating force behind the effort to bring knowledge to your fellow man in every possible discipline.

...we realize that "all of us have knowledge"; knowledge inflates with pride, but love builds up.

— 1 Cor 8: 1 —

God's Greatest Gift

God wants us to use our intellect and present to him in prayer our political, social, economic, technological, and ecological problems. We have to take our intellect, beautiful as it is, into the heart, to wash from it all the erroneous ideas and temptations that beset us 24 hours a day. This is so difficult that it is factually impossible, except in the heart of the Lord.

On the one hand, we must use our mind to the fullest. On the other hand, we need moments when the wings of the intellect are closed, and the soul, passive and emptied of all thought, listens lovingly to the Spirit for confirmation of such knowledge as has been arrived at.

Then a new light is shed upon each area, a new slant given. Then is added that extra grace of God's wisdom that alone will bless and enhance all human thinking!

The light of the Holy Spirit is ours. Why shouldn't he illuminate and lead us toward a solution to the problems that confront humanity today?

"Whoever remains in me and I in him will bear much fruit, because without me you can do nothing."

— Jn 15: 5 —

Faith For All Cultures

You are growing in grace and wisdom and prayer and all the things that God desires for you. But the faith that cuts through everything, the faith that is like a sword, the faith that expects a miracle – there you have difficulty.

Because of your environment and culture, you have difficulty with this faith. God cannot be unaware of the American-Canadian cultural patterns. So if he is aware of these patterns, he has to do something.

Now we should stop being wrongly cultural. We should bring our culture in its beauty regarding God, but not in its ugliness. We need to stop saying, "Well, we're just different." Of course, we are different! But faith isn't different. Faith is the same for the Russian, for the American, for everybody. Faith is a light!

"The kingdom of heaven is like a mustard seed that a person took and sowed in a field. It is the smallest of all the seeds, yet when full-grown it is the largest of plants. It becomes a large bush, and the 'birds of the sky come and dwell in its branches.'"

— Mt 13: 31-32 —

Growing In Faith

Those who desire to preach the Gospel with their lives must pray for growth in faith. Without faith we cannot do it.

And if we have faith in God we must have faith in man – even the most evil among us has some redeeming feature. Faith will seek it out.

For a time, you who set out on this quest may not be able to hear, to see. But suddenly you will be mysteriously visited. A hand will touch your ears and they will be opened, not only to the speech of man but to the speech of God. A hand will touch your eyes and you will see, not only with the eyes of man but with the sight of God.

"Lord, behold, we are kneeling here together, beseeching you to give us an increase of faith. Let our hearts be open to you."

...whoever is begotten by God conquers the world. And the victory that conquers the world is our faith.

— 1 Jn 5: 4 —

Beginning Again

Every year is a special year, and every day is the acceptable time for beginning again.

Let us begin by purging our souls from all that has made us tepid and brought down about us the ruin of our house, built so flimsily on the sands of worldliness. Let us purge our souls of complacency, tepidity, and indifference. Let us cease our worship of self, of gold and silver, and of material security.

Only through Christ's Redemption can man begin to live again. Only through the holy sacrament of penance can he rise from the dead, and begin once more to live in God!

Renewing our baptismal vows, let us begin again the ascent to Christ via his commandments, his beatitudes, and his counsels of perfection. Let us walk this royal road to him, lightly burdened, busy only about his business, burning with zeal for his house.

Let us do this through Mary, his Mother.

There is still time to restore this world and all that dwell therein to him who created and owns it. Unless we do begin again, we shall surely perish.

Maranatha — Come, Lord, we need you so.

Keep on doing what you have learned and received and heard and seen in me. Then the God of peace will be with you.

— Phil 4: 9

SOURCES

BOOKS:
Dearly Beloved, Vol. 2
Faith
The Gospel Without Compromise
Grace in Every Season
Living the Gospel Without Compromise
Where Love Is God Is

OTHER SOURCES:
Articles
Correspondence
Diary
Local Directors' Meetings
Spiritual Readings at Madonna House
Staff Letters
Staff Meetings

To find out about the progress of Catherine Doherty's cause for canonization in the Catholic Church, please visit the web site:

www.catherinedoherty.org

To learn more about the life and work of the world-wide Madonna House Apostolate founded by Catherine Doherty, please visit:

www.madonnahouse.org

Also by Catherine Doherty and available from Madonna House Publications:

Beginning Again
Bogoroditza
Donkey Bells: Advent and Christmas
Fragments of my Life
Grace in Every Season
In the Footprints of Loneliness
In the Furnace of Doubts
Living the Gospel Without Compromise
Not Without Parables
On the Cross of Rejection
Poustinia
Sobornost
Soul of my Soul
Strannik
The Gospel Without Compromise
Uródivoi: Holy Fools

Audio Books on CD by Catherine Doherty:

Fragments of My Life
Not Without Parables
Poustinia
Sobornost
Strannik

Catherine Doherty was fond of saying,

"With God, every moment is the moment of beginning again."

...and now you can experience a new "moment of grace" each day at home or in the office with our perpetual desk calendar. It has a quotation for each day of the year from the writings, diaries, talks and extraordinary spiritual life of Catherine Doherty. It is arranged by date, and notes the major fixed feasts and saints' days every year.

For anyone looking for a deeper insight into the meaning of daily life in Christ, this 5¼" x 4¼" perpetual desk calendar makes a wonderful gift for any occasion!

370 pages • ISBN 0-921440-56-1

These and other titles by Catherine Doherty can be ordered directly from Madonna House Publications by calling toll free:

1-888-703-7110

MADONNA HOUSE PUBLICATIONS
COMBERMERE • ONTARIO • CANADA • K0J 1L0

"Lord, give bread to the hungry, and hunger for you to those who have bread," was a favourite prayer of our foundress, Catherine Doherty. At Madonna House Publications, we strive to satisfy the spiritual hunger for God in our modern world with the timeless words of the Gospel message.

Faithful to the teachings of the Catholic Church and its magisterium, Madonna House Publications is a non-profit apostolate dedicated to publishing high quality and easily accessible books, audiobooks, videos and music. We pray our publications will awaken and deepen in our readers an experience of Jesus' love in the most simple and ordinary facets of everyday life.

Your generosity can help Madonna House Publications provide the poor around the world with editions of important spiritual works containing the enduring wisdom of the Gospel message. If you would like to help, please send your contribution to the address below. We also welcome your questions and comments. May God bless you for your participation in this apostolate.

    Madonna House Publications
    2888 Dafoe Rd, RR 2
    Combermere ON K0J 1L0
    Canada

Internet: www.madonnahouse.org/publications

E-mail: publications@madonnahouse.org

Telephone: (613) 756-3728

This seasonal devotional features meditations drawn from the down-to-earth and eminently practical writings of Catherine Doherty.

Providing daily spiritual guidance, there are deep insights on prayer and spiritual growth as well as homespun words of advice on everyday work and family life.

"A sampling of daily topics evokes their richness and variety:
- Remedy for Pain: Forgiveness
- What Christ Asks of Us
- What Happens When You Take the Risk
- Superficial Communications and Loneliness
- The Gospel Is Risky Business
- A Meditation on Yelling

Because *Grace in Every Season* lives up to its title, it also makes a wonderful spiritual gift for any occasion: Christmas, birthday, graduation, wedding, or anniversary."

— Larry Holley, *Book Nook*

"The writings of Catherine Doherty belong in the realm of contemporary classics. With this book of seasonal selections, we have ready-at-hand some of her most memorable reflections on the mysteries of our faith as well as personal accounts of her profound prayer experiences. I heartily recommend it for all Christians."

— Susan Muto, author *Pathways to Living*

320 pages
ISBN 0-921440-31-6